THE VIETNAM WAR

1964-1975 DAY BY DAY

Ian Westwell

BROWN BEAR BOOKS

Published by Brown Bear Books Limited

An imprint of
The Brown Reference Group plc
68 Topstone Road
Redding
Connecticut
06896
USA
www.brownreference.com

ISBN: 978-1-933834-23-8

Designers: Basil UK Ltd
Creative Director: Jeni Child
Children's Publisher: Anne O'Daly
Editorial Director: Lindsey Lowe
Design Manager: Sarah Williams
Editor: Peter Darman

Printed in China

Photographic credits:
All photographs **U.S. National Archives** except the following:
Robert Hunt Library: 6 (both), 8, 10 (bottom), 16 (bottom), 28 (bottom),
29, 33, 38 (bottom), 41, 42 (bottom), 44 (bottom).

Contents

Introduction

The area of the world that is now called Southeast Asia was once called Indochina. This word was thought up in the 1820s by a Danish map maker called Konrad Malte-Brun. Indochina included the states of Tonkin, Annam, Cochin-China, Laos, and Cambodia.

All these states were ruled by local kings and emperors. Modern-day Vietnam was formed from Tonkin, Annam, and Cochin-China.

The first Europeans to arrive in Indochina were Catholic priests in the 17th century. In the 19th century the local rulers wanted to get rid of the Catholic priests. The priests were trying to get the local people to go their churches. But the French protected the priests and sent warships to the area to threaten the local rulers. In 1862, Emperor Tu Duc of Vietnam was forced to sign a treaty with France. This treaty protected the priests and gave France the right to trade in the area.

The French take over

Over the next 20 years the French sent more ships and people to the region. Indochina was rich in gold and silver, precious stones, coal, tin, exotic woods, silk, spices, and rice. That is why the French were so eager to control the area. By 1887 they ruled most of Indochina.

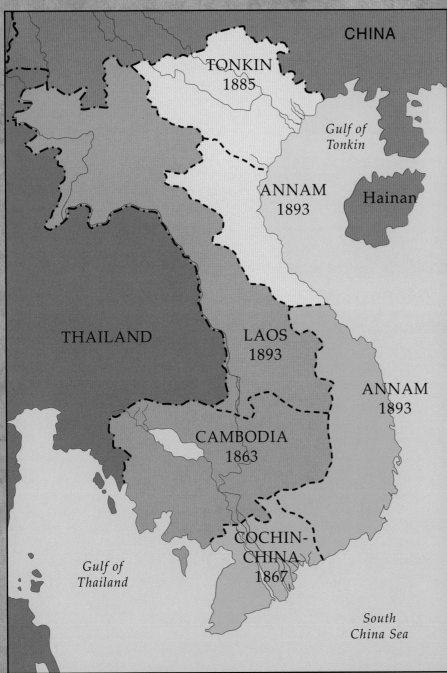

CHINA

TONKIN
1885

Gulf of
Tonkin

ANNAM
1893

Hainan

THAILAND

LAOS
1893

ANNAM
1893

CAMBODIA
1863

COCHIN-
CHINA
1867

Gulf of
Thailand

South
China Sea

The French conquest of Indochina in the 19th century. The dates show the year when the French took over each region. By the end of the 19th century the whole area was called French Indochina.

The French decided to make the area part of their empire. So in 1887 they created what was called French Indochina. By the end of the 19th century there were 50,000 French people living in Indochina. The local people worked hard, but they were poor. There were few schools to send their children to. And the French treated the locals as second-class citizens. These things made the local people angry. They rose up against the French many times between 1930 and 1931. But they were easily crushed by the French army.

World War II
World War II broke out in 1939, and in 1940 France was defeated by Germany in Europe. Some French soldiers remained in Indochina. But in 1945 Japan, which was very strong in the Pacific region, took over Indochina. Japan was on the losing side when World War II ended in September 1945, though. France then thought it could take back Indochina. But local communists under their leader Ho Chi Minh wanted to control the country for themselves.

Ho Chi Minh and the communists
The communists had the support of many Vietnamese, who were tired of being ruled by foreigners. Ho Chi Minh had declared himself president of Vietnam in August 1945. Then French troops arrived in the south of the country in October 1945 to take back control of Vietnam. They took over the south of the country, but Ho Chi Minh and his communists controlled the north.

Ho Chi Minh became president of the north of the country in January 1946. The north became a new country. It was called the Democratic Republic of Vietnam. The French created another country in the south. They called it the Republic of Cochin-China. This country would later be called South Vietnam. The communist north was later called North Vietnam. The French wanted to control the whole of Vietnam, and so did the communists. War broke out between the two sides in December 1946. The French lost, but then the Americans arrived to support the South. The fighting would continue until 1975.

These are the main towns and cities in South Vietnam. The capital of the country was Saigon. The Americans built camps for their soldiers at Khe Sanh and Da Nang.

French reinforcements parachute into Dien Bien Phu.

OCTOBER 6, 1945, Indochina

French troops arrive in the city of Saigon. Japan has been defeated in World War II. The French are determined to take control of Indochina again.

MARCH 6, 1946, Indochina

Ho Chi Minh signs an agreement with the French. This recognizes Ho as president of the Democratic Republic of Vietnam, later called North Vietnam. It is a communist state. The French set up a separate state in the south. It is called the Republic of Cochin-Chain, later called South Vietnam.

MARCH 10, 1945, Indochina

The Japanese arrest all the French administrators and military personnel in Indochina. This is what the French call the area that would become Vietnam.

DECEMBER 19, 1946, Indochina

War breaks out between France and North Vietnam. It is called the First Indochina War.

AUGUST 16, 1945, Indochina

The Vietnamese nationalist leader Ho Chi Minh declares himself president of Vietnam. He arrives in Hanoi on August 19.

MARCH 20, 1954, United States

American leaders discuss aiding the French in Indochina. French forces are surrounded in North Vietnam at a place called Dien Bien

TURNING POINTS: Dien Bien Phu

Dien Bien Phu was the place where the French set up a base in late 1953. It was in North Vietnam and behind enemy lines. The French wanted to use the base to attack Ho Chi Minh's communists. But in March 1954 the North Vietnamese surrounded the base and laid siege to it. The French were unable to get supplies to the 16,000 men there. On May 7, 1954, the French garrison surrendered. More than 2,200 French troops had died.

NVA – North Vietnamese Army.

6

EYEWITNESS: Archie Clapp, U.S. Marine, 1962

"The VC (Viet Cong) ambushed a convoy to the north of Saigon, killed two American officers and several Vietnamese soldiers, and captured a quantity of weapons. The squadron was diverted from another mission to land troops in an attempt to head them off. The helicopters received heavy small-arms fire. As soon as they had discharged their troops, a radio call was received that requested them to land again and move some troops."

Phu. The Americans are considering air strikes against the communist besiegers.

MAY 7, 1954, North Vietnam
Dien Bien Phu falls to the Viet Minh. The French have lost 35,000 men in the war. They are forced to leave Vietnam.

JANUARY 1, 1955, South Vietnam
U.S. advisors arrive to help the South Vietnamese. They will train the Vietnamese armed forces. The United States does not want South Vietnam falling to North Vietnam, which is a communist regime.

JANUARY, 1958, South Vietnam
North Vietnam has decided it wants to take over South Vietnam. It orders communist guerrillas operating in South Vietnam to begin attacking people and property.

DECEMBER, 1960, North Vietnam
North Vietnam forms the *Viet Nam Cong San* (Vietnamese communists) to fight in South

Vietnam. This group will become known as the Viet Cong.

AUGUST 2, 1961, United States
President Kennedy says that the United States will do all it can to support and save South Vietnam from the communists.

FEBRUARY 7, 1962, South Vietnam
There are now 4,000 American military personnel in South Vietnam. They are training the South's soldiers.

A U.S. advisor trains South Vietnamese soldiers.

ARVN – Army of the Republic of Vietnam (South Vietnam).

7

Buddhists protesting in Saigon.

NOVEMBER 1, 1963, South Vietnam

A group of army generals organizes a military coup against the Diem regime. Rebels lay siege to the presidential palace in Saigon, which is captured by the following morning. President Diem is shot dead by the rebels.

NOVEMBER 22, 1963, United States

President John F. Kennedy is assassinated while visiting Dallas, Texas, with his wife. Vice President Lyndon B. Johnson takes over as president.

NOVEMBER 24, 1963, United States

President Lyndon B. Johnson states that the United States will continue to support South Vietnam.

MAY 16, 1962, Thailand

President Kennedy announces that troops will be sent to Thailand. This is in response to a request from the government of Thailand. Thailand is being attacked by Communist units in Laos. Communist military units are moving toward the Thai/Vietnamese border.

JANUARY 2, 1963, South Vietnam

At the village of Ap Bac around 2,500 ARVN soldiers suffer a humiliating defeat at the hands of the Viet Cong. The ARVN soldiers had been armed and equipped by the United States.

JULY 17, 1963, South Vietnam

South Vietnamese policeman put down a riot by 1,000 Buddhists. The Buddhists are protesting religious discrimination by the government. President Kennedy says that a religious crisis in South Vietnam is interfering with the fight against the Viet Cong. He hopes that President Diem and the Buddhist leaders will reach an agreement on respecting the rights of others in the country.

EYEWITNESS:
Le Ly Hayslip, Viet Cong

"The children were organized into committees to watch for informers and to run messages between the villagers and the Viet Cong in the field. The able-bodied men who were excused from duty with the guerrilla militia were organized into labor squads to dig tunnels that would allow the Viet Cong to pass into and out of the village unseen. Families were ordered to build bunkers."

Military coup – revolt by soldiers.

JANUARY 18, 1964, South Vietnam

The ARVN is transported into battle by 115 assault helicopters, the largest airlift of the war in Vietnam to date. Some 1,100 ARVN soldiers are airlifted into the critical War Zone D region north of Bien Hoa. The Viet Cong withdraws from the area.

FEBRUARY 7 South Vietnam

A Viet Cong bomb planted in Saigon's Capital-Kinh Do Theater kills three and wounds 50 Americans. American families are sheltering in the theater. The Viet Cong also explodes other bombs in the city.

APRIL 25 South Vietnam

General William C. Westmoreland officially takes command of Military Assistance Command, Vietnam (MACV). He leads all American forces in the country.

AUGUST South Vietnam

The Viet Cong (VC) holds the military initiative in South Vietnam. They are supported by regular army units from North Vietnam. The VC and North Vietnamese Army (NVA) now control much of the countryside in South Vietnam.

AUGUST 2 Gulf of Tonkin

North Vietnamese torpedo boats attack the USS *Maddox* (a destroyer) in the Gulf of Tonkin. President Johnson warns the communists that U.S. ships "will take whatever steps are necessary that are appropriate for their defense."

South Vietnamese climb out of a CH-21 helicopter.

CH-21 – American tandem rotor helicopter used in Vietnam until 1964.

A captured Viet Cong member.

AUGUST 5 North Vietnam

American aircraft bomb North Vietnam. This is in retaliation for the attack on U.S. ships in the Gulf of Tonkin. The U.S. planes severely damage the North Vietnamese gunboat and torpedo fleet, destroying 8 and damaging 21 others. Smoke from the petroleum storage areas rises 14,000 ft (4,267 m) into the air. The North Vietnamese shoot down two American jets.

AUGUST 5 North Vietnam

The United States Congress approves the Southeast Asia Resolution. (The Senate votes 88-2, and House of Representatives 414-0). This is the so-called "Gulf of Tonkin Resolution." It allows President Johnson to take all the steps that are necessary to protect U.S. personnel and U.S. interests within Vietnam.

OCTOBER South Vietnam

The 1,300-man 5th Special Forces Group, or Green Berets, arrives in Vietnam. Its purpose is to assist the South Vietnamese government against the communists.

NOVEMBER South Vietnam

North Vietnamese premier Pham Van Dong visits the Soviet Union. He asks the Russian communists for military aid. This includes antiaircraft defenses to protect the North against American jets.

KEY PEOPLE: Viet Cong

Viet Cong is short for *Viet Nam Cong San*, which means Vietnamese communists. The Viet Cong (at right) fought in South Vietnam against the South Vietnamese and the Americans. They were not part of the regular North Vietnamese Army. The Viet Cong fought a terrorist war. They used small units to take control of the countryside. They suffered terrible casualties during the 1968 Tet Offensive (see page 22). After 1968 the Viet Cong was made up of North Vietnamese Army soldiers.

Green Beret – a member of the U.S. Special Forces.

EYEWITNESS: Sergeant Bill East, Saigon, 1963

"We encountered several anti-American demonstrations. During one riot, I was on duty by myself in the embassy annex. The riot lasted three days and nights. There was a locker with several weapons stored there. I loaded all of them. I took a position on a balcony inside the front iron gate, and stayed there each night, when the crowds were the heaviest and rowdiest. During the day I would get some sleep, or rummage for something to eat."

NOVEMBER South Vietnam

Two Viet Cong and NVA regiments attack the ARVN in Binh Dinh Province. This is the second largest province in South Vietnam. ARVN forces are driven back into their fortified camps. The Viet Cong win control of the countryside. By the end of October the Viet Cong control most of the province. The South Vietnamese government is limited to some towns in the province and its capital city, Qui Nhon.

NOVEMBER 3 United States

Lyndon B. Johnson is elected president of the United States. He wins a landslide victory over Senator Barry Goldwater (Republican, Arizona).

DECEMBER 24 South Vietnam

Viet Cong guerrillas set off a terrorist bomb. It explodes in the Brinks Bachelor Officer's Quarters in downtown Saigon. Two Americans are killed and 52 are wounded.

DECEMBER 31 South Vietnam

There are now 23,000 U.S. officers and men and women in South Vietnam. They are from the army, air force, marines, and navy. The number of Americans in the South is growing larger each month.

DECEMBER 31 North Vietnam

American intelligence reports that there are 12,500 North Vietnamese military personnel fighting in South Vietnam. This is a lot more than in 1963. It shows that the communists are increasing their efforts to take over South Vietnam.

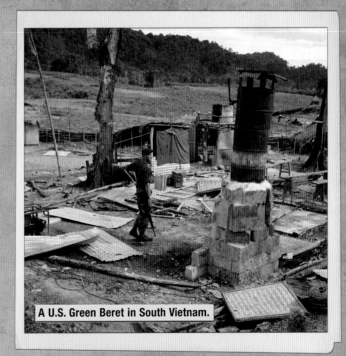

A U.S. Green Beret in South Vietnam.

Guerrillas – soldiers who do not wear uniforms.

U.S. Marines land at Da Nang.

JANUARY 8, 1965, South Korea

The South Korean government sends 2,000 military advisors to South Vietnam. This is to assist U.S. military personnel in training the South Vietnamese Armed Forces.

FEBRUARY 13 North Vietnam

The Americans begin Operation Rolling Thunder. This is a program of air attacks against North Vietnam.

FEBRUARY 15 China

The communist Chinese government warns that it will enter the war in Vietnam if American troops invade North Vietnam.

MARCH 6 South Vietnam

The first big units of U.S. ground troops arrive in South Vietnam. Two battalions of U.S. Marines land at Da Nang to guard the U.S. air facility that is based there.

APRIL 7 United States

President Johnson offers North Vietnam a $1-billion U.S. aid program to develop the Mekong Delta region and Southeast Asia. In return he wants North Vietnam to stop trying to take over South Vietnam. If North Vietnam agrees, the war will be over.

APRIL 11 North Vietnam

North Vietnam turns down Johnson's offer. The North believes it can defeat the Americans in South Vietnam.

KEY WEAPONS: Helicopters

Vietnam was the first helicopter war. Helicopters such as the UH-34 (at right) were used to take soldiers into battle. They also provided fire support for ground troops. The workhorse of the war was the UH-1 Huey. It was used to transport troops and take away the wounded. The U.S. cargo helicopter was the CH-47 Chinook. In total, the Americans lost 10 helicopters over North Vietnam and 2,066 over South Vietnam. Another 2,566 were lost in accidents.

Draft – being forced to join the army.

SEPTEMBER 18 South Vietnam

A battalion from the 1st Brigade, 101st Airborne Division, begins operations in the rugged Son Con Valley, 18 miles (29 km) northeast of An Khe. The Viet Cong is hard hit by about 100 air strikes and 11,000 rounds of artillery. It begins to slip away. The Viet Cong use "hugging" tactics. These prevent the Americans from using either close-in air support or massive artillery fire without putting themselves in danger.

A napalm strike against the Viet Cong.

OCTOBER 14 United States

The U.S. Defense Department orders a military draft call for 45,224 men for December. This is the largest number of men drafted since the Korean War in 1950.

OCTOBER 15–16 United States

The student-run National Coordinating Committee To End the War in Vietnam sponsors a series of nationwide demonstrations against the Vietnam War on colleges and campuses and in major U.S. cities.

OCTOBER 19 South Vietnam

The North Vietnamese Army (NVA) opens its campaign against the Americans. Its troops attack the Plei Mei U.S. Special Forces camp, 25 miles (40 km) northwest of Pleiku. The attack fails. The NVA will carry out many more attacks against the Americans before the end of the year.

OCTOBER 23 South Vietnam

There are now 148,300 American troops in South Vietnam. Some 830 Americans have so far been killed in combat.

EYEWITNESS: Lieutenant Caputo, Da Nang, 1965

"Something finally did happen that morning, and when it did I near jumped out of my skin. It wasn't much, a burst of heavy rifle fire from the head of the column. The shooting lasted no more than a few seconds, and then I heard my heart drumming against my chest. I ran forward at a crouch, weaving around prone marines. From the ridge, a sniper had opened up on the point. Although the sniper had broken contact, we suspected an ambush."

Napalm – a fuel and gel mixture used in aircraft bombs.

OCTOBER 27 South Vietnam

The Korean Capital (Tiger) Division arrives in South Vietnam.

NOVEMBER 4 South Vietnam

The Battle of the Ia Drang Valley. For 35 days the U.S. 1st Cavalry division pursues and fights the North Vietnamese 32d, 33rd, and 66th Regiments. The North Vietnamese suffer heavy casualties and return to base in Cambodia. When the fighting ends, 60 percent of the Americans are casualties. One in three soldiers in the battalions have been killed or wounded.

NOVEMBER 27 South Vietnam

The South Vietnamese Army suffers a major defeat. The ARVN 7th Regiment fights the Viet Cong's 271st Regiment. The battle takes place in the Michelin Rubber Plantation northwest of Saigon. The ARVN 7th Regiment suffers very heavy casualties.

U.S. Marines on patrol in South Vietnam.

DECEMBER 15 North Vietnam

U.S. Air Force aircraft bomb and destroy a North Vietnamese power plant at Uongbi. It is the first American air raid on a major North Vietnamese industrial target.

DECEMBER 23 South Vietnam

Troops of the U.S. 1st Infantry Division destroy a large amount of Viet Cong ammunition near Saigon.

KEY PEOPLE: Ho Chi Minh

Ho Chi Minh means "He Who Enlightens." He was a communist who first fought to free Vietnam from the French. When the French left, Vietnam was divided into North and South. Ho became president of the communist North. As leader of the North he organized the fight against South Vietnam and the Americans. Ho did not live to see the end of the war. He died in September 1969. When North Vietnam won the war in 1975, Saigon was renamed Ho Chi Minh City in his honor.

Airmobile troops – soldiers who ride in helicopters.

EYEWITNESS: Jack Smith, Ia Drang, 1965

"It felt as if a white-hot sledgehammer had hit the right side of my face. Then something hit my left leg. I lost consciousness. I came out of it feeling intense pain in my leg and a numbness in my head. Blood was pouring down my forehead and filling my eyeglasses. It was also pouring out of my mouth. I slapped a bandage on the side of my face and tied it around my head. I felt better. I decided it was time to get out."

JANUARY 4, 1966, South Vietnam

The Viet Cong and North Vietnamese Army (NVA) attack a U.S. Army Special Forces camp at Khe Sanh in Quang Tri Province. The Viet Cong use Soviet 120mm mortars. This is the heaviest weapon yet used in the Vietnam War by the North Vietnamese.

MARCH 4–8 South Vietnam

Operation Utah. This is a combined operation involving U.S. Marines and South Vietnamese troops. The fighting takes place near Quang Ngai City. The NVA's 36th Regiment loses one-third of its strength.

APRIL 24 South Vietnam

The U.S. 1st Infantry Division enters War Zone C near the Cambodian border in Tay Ninh Province. This is the first major Allied (American and South Vietnamese) move into the enemy stronghold since 1962. The American soldiers uncover vast quantities of arms, clothing, medicine, and other supplies.

JULY 7–AUGUST 2 South Vietnam

Operation Hastings, the largest military action so far in the war. It takes place 55 miles (88 km) northwest of Hue, near the Demilitarized Zone (DMZ). Over a period of 28 days, the U.S. Marines and South Vietnamese troops kill more than 882 Viet Cong members.

AUGUST 1–25 South Vietnam

Operation Paul Revere in Pleiku Province. This results in 809 communist deaths.

Huey helicopters in South Vietnam.

Battalion – a unit of 500 soldiers.

U.S. Marines crossing a stream in South Vietnam.

AUGUST 6–21 South Vietnam

Operation Colorado begins. This is a combined U.S. Marine and South Vietnamese Army operation. It is in Quang Nam/Quang Tin Provinces. In the 16-day operation, 674 Viet Cong are killed.

SEPTEMBER 11 South Vietnam

The people of South Vietnam vote to elect a new government. Over 80 percent of those who register vote in polling places throughout South Vietnam.

SEPTEMBER–NOVEMBER South Vietnam

Operation Attleboro begins in War Zone C, Tay Ninh Province. It lasts for 72 days. It is started by the 196th Light Infantry Brigade. When it ends, there are 1,106 confirmed communist casualties. This is the largest number of enemy dead recorded to date as the result of a U.S. military operation.

SEPTEMBER 23 South Vietnam

Operation Maeng Ho is conducted by the élite Republic of Korea Capital Division. It operates in Binh Dinh Province and lasts for 48 days. The Korean soldiers kill more than 1,161 enemy soldiers in this operation.

OCTOBER 2–24 South Vietnam

Operation Irving is carried out by the sky soldiers of the U.S. 1st Cavalry Division (Airmobile), South Vietnamese, and Republic of Korea troops. It lasts for a total

KEY PEOPLE: Lyndon B. Johnson

Born in 1908, Johnson became president in 1963 after President Kennedy was assassinated. During his administration he signed into law the Civil Rights Acts (1964). This was the best civil rights legislation since the Reconstruction era after the Civil War. He was very unpopular for sending more American troops to Vietnam. He asked for peace talks in 1968 but did not live to see the end of the war. He died of a heart attack on January 22, 1973.

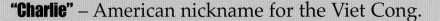

"Charlie" – American nickname for the Viet Cong.

EYEWITNESS: John J. McGinty, Operation Hastings, 1966

"We started getting mortar fire, followed by automatic weapons fire from all sides. They were blowing bugles, and we could see them waving flags. 'Charlie' moved in waves with small arms right behind the mortars, and we estimated we were being attacked by a thousand men. We just couldn't kill them fast enough. My squads were cut off from each other, and together we were cut off from the rest of the company. I had men in the high grass."

of 23 days. It is fought against the North Vietnamese Army (NVA) 610th Division in Binh Dinh Province. At the end there are 681 enemy casualties.

OCTOBER 24–25 The Philippines

At a conference in Manila, U.S. president Johnson meets with leaders from six other nations: South Vietnam, New Zealand, Australia, Korea, Thailand, and the Philippines. The leaders issue a statement called the *Declaration of Peace*. It demands the peaceful end to the Vietnam War. The North Vietnamese ignore the statement.

OCTOBER 25 South Vietnam

Operation Thayer I begins. This is an operation in Binh Dinh Province. There is a total of 1,757 confirmed enemy casualties, and the operation lasts for 111 days.

NOVEMBER 30 South Vietnam

The beginning of Operation Fairfax in and around Saigon. During this 380-day operation, U.S. and South Vietnamese soldiers inflict a total of 1,043 casualties on the Viet Cong enemy.

DECEMBER 6 United States

Keeping South Vietnam safe is proving expensive. The Johnson administration in Washington says that it will need an extra $9 billion to $10 billion in funding to pay for the war in Vietnam during the current financial year.

B-52 Stratofortresses bombing the Viet Cong.

B-52 – American eight-engined jet bomber.

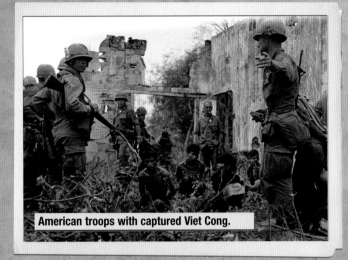

American troops with captured Viet Cong.

JANUARY 8, 1967, South Vietnam

The U.S. Army launches Operation Cedar Falls. This aims to destroy the Viet Cong in the so-called "Iron Triangle," an area near Saigon. Cedar Falls ran throughout January and into February. U.S. troops destroyed hundreds of enemy fortifications, captured large quantities of supplies and food, and evacuated villages. Many Viet Cong fled from the area.

FEBRUARY South Vietnam

The North Vietnamese are sending many soldiers and weapons to South Vietnam.

FEBRUARY 21 South Vietnam

Operation Junction City. This is designed to stop communist forces escaping into nearby Cambodia. Elements of the 173rd Airborne Brigade make the only paratroop drop of the Vietnam War. Near Route 13 there are violent battles. The communist forces try to defeat U.S. units and help their comrades flee into Cambodia.

MARCH 2 South Vietnam

Two U.S. Air Force fighter jets mistakenly bomb the village of Lang Vei. This kills 112 Vietnamese civilians and wounds 213. It also destroys 140 buildings.

MARCH 18 South Vietnam

The first woman U.S. Marine is assigned to United States Military Assistance Command

TURNING POINTS: Search and Destroy

"Search and destroy" was an American tactic. It was used in Vietnam to kill communists. Troops in helicopters would "search" for enemy units. After finding them they would land and "destroy" them. They would be supported by massive amounts of artillery and air power. It was an aggressive tactic, but it failed. This was because it was the communists who chose the time and place of battle. "Search and destroy" was abandoned in 1968.

Artillery – cannons or mortars.

EYEWITNESS: Lewis Walt, U.S. Marine, 1967

"Each day we free more people and have more South Vietnamese thankful for the protection we are giving them. I talked with an elderly lady through an interpreter. She and her family have been under VC domination for nearly 10 years. She lost both her husband and some of her children as a result of VC tactics. She told me that she had lived in terror during these years and was so grateful that the Marines had liberated her."

Headquarters in Saigon. Master Sergeant Barbara J. Dulinsky will serve at General Westmoreland's headquarters in the combat operations center.

MARCH 19 South Vietnam
Operation Junction City. Fire Support Base Gold, near Souoi Da, is nearly wiped out by the Viet Cong. A fire base is a camp that has lots of artillery that can fire at the enemy. The Americans fight back. U.S. soldiers fire straight at the enemy with "Beehive" artillery rounds. These contain hundreds of tiny metal darts. More than 600 Viet Cong are killed.

APRIL 24 South Vietnam
A major battle breaks out between the U.S. Marines and the North Vietnamese Army (NVA) near the marine Khe Sanh fire base. This is near the border with North Vietnam.

MAY 1 South Vietnam
There are now 436,000 American military men and women serving in South Vietnam.

MAY 11 South Vietnam
The First Battle of Khe Sanh ends. The U.S. Marines are defending a fire base. They beat off a furious NVA attack. During the fighting, the 1st Marine Aircraft Wing flies more than 1,110 sorties. U.S. Marine and army artillery units fire more than 25,000 rounds at the enemy to support the U.S. Marines in and around Khe Sanh. The North Vietnamese Army loses 940 men. Marine losses are 155 dead.

In the Mekong Delta the Americans set up the Brown Water Navy to patrol the waterways.

"Grunt" – nickname for an American soldier.

JUNE 17 South Vietnam

American strength in Vietnam is 450,000 men and women. The total strength of the Vietnamese Armed Forces is 600,000. Other Free World forces total 54,000 troops. The Viet Cong has an estimated 260,000 troops.

JULY 14 South Vietnam

During the night, Viet Cong rocket units move out of "Happy Valley," southwest of Da Nang. They open fire against the American base at Da Nang, destroying many aircraft.

Viet Cong suspects are rounded up.

AUGUST 13–19 North Vietnam

U.S. Air Force B-52 bombers carry out hundreds of raids against North Vietnam. Targets include troops, industrial sites, railroads, and truck depots.

AUGUST 27 South Vietnam

In the Mekong Delta region the Viet Cong launches a series of raids against South Vietnamese civilians in Cantho and Hojan, 30 miles (48 km) south of Hue, the ancient capital of Vietnam.

OCTOBER 8 South Vietnam

The new Huey Cobra (AH-1G) helicopter enters the fighting for the first time. It has been designed specially to support ground troops. It is armed with rockets and guns.

KEY PEOPLE: William Westmoreland

General Westmoreland, born in 1914, commanded American forces in the Vietnam War. He planned to win the war by seeking out and destroying the communists on the ground, and by bombing North Vietnam. He hoped the bombing would stop North Vietnam sending troops into the South. But the North continued to support communists in South Vietnam. And U.S. troops failed to destroy the Viet Cong on the ground. William Westmoreland died in 2005.

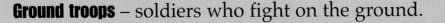

Ground troops – soldiers who fight on the ground.

NOVEMBER 2 South Vietnam

The Viet Cong launches a series of raids against the refugee settlements at Dai Luc and Hieu Duc, 15 miles (24 km) southwest of Da Nang. Some 22 South Vietnamese civilians are killed in the attack, while 42 are wounded, and 57 are missing. The enemy raids destroy 559 houses and leave 625 Vietnamese families homeless.

Huey Cobra gunships in Vietnam.

NOVEMBER 14 South Vietnam

U.S. Marine Major General Bruno A. Hocmuth, commanding general of the 3rd Marine Division, is killed. His UH-1E helicopter explodes and crashes near Dong Ha, 5 miles (8 km) northwest of Hue City.

DECEMBER 8 South Vietnam

In one of the largest single battles yet to occur in the Mekong Delta, the South Vietnamese 21st Infantry Division traps the Viet Cong. A battle takes place 100 miles (160 km) southwest of Saigon. The Viet Cong loses 365 dead.

DECEMBER 31 South Vietnam

U.S. Army strength in South Vietnam is now 320,000 troops. The U.S. Navy has 31,000, and the U.S. Air Force has 56,000. The U.S. Marines have a force of 78,000 and the U.S. Coast Guard has a force of 1,200. Free World forces in South Vietnam include: 6,182 Australians; 47,800 South Koreans; 516 New Zealanders; 2,020 from the Philippines; and 2,205 officers and men from Thailand.

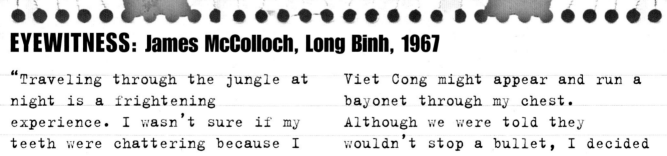

EYEWITNESS: James McColloch, Long Binh, 1967

"Traveling through the jungle at night is a frightening experience. I wasn't sure if my teeth were chattering because I was cold or afraid. I tried to ignore the knowledge that I might step on a booby trap or that the Viet Cong might appear and run a bayonet through my chest. Although we were told they wouldn't stop a bullet, I decided to zip up my flak jacket as I walked and increased my grip on the rifle."

Free World forces – foreign units supporting South Vietnam.

American troops cross a stream in Vietnam.

JANUARY 23, 1968, Gulf of Tonkin

The communist North Koreans seize the American intelligence-gathering ship USS *Pueblo* off the coast of Korea.

JANUARY 27 Vietnam

A seven-day ceasefire for the Tet (New Year) holiday begins. However, the communists plan to break the ceasefire and attack South Vietnam.

JANUARY 30 South Vietnam

In pre-dawn assaults, the North Vietnamese Army (NVA) and Viet Cong launch attacks throughout South Vietnam. This is the start of the Tet Offensive.

JANUARY 31 South Vietnam

Viet Cong troops attack the U.S. Embassy in Saigon and seize the building. They hold part of it for six hours. U.S. Marine embassy guards and U.S. Army military policemen retake the building. They kill all enemy soldiers that have managed to enter the embassy.

FEBRUARY 23 South Vietnam

North Vietnamese artillery gunners and mortars fire more than 1,300 shells at the U.S. Marine garrison in Khe Sanh. This will be the heaviest shelling of the Marine base during the siege of Khe Sanh. Khe Sanh is an isolated base near the border with North Vietnam. It is very vulnerable to attack.

TURNING POINTS: My Lai massacre

In March 1968, American troops killed 300 people in the village of My Lai, South Vietnam. The soldiers, who also burnt the village (at right), were angry because many of their comrades had been killed and injured in the area. The American public did not know about this event until November 1969. Many questioned the conduct of American soldiers in Vietnam. The leader of the soldiers at My Lai was Lieutenant Calley. He was given a life sentence for the killings, but was released in 1974.

Ceasefire – a halt in the fighting.

EYEWITNESS: George Carver, U.S. Marine Corps, 1968

"We are dirty, muddy, wet, and a bit discouraged. The rains have left us but the heat is overwhelming. Very hectic last night. We shot and wounded one marine and captured two VC suspects. All three were about 600 yards in front of our perimeter. The marine should have known better than to be out there after dark anyway. I feel very little remorse for him, as he was careless and stupid. He's lucky he only got one in the leg."

MARCH 2 South Vietnam
Operation Hue City ends successfully. The 1st and 5th Marines defeat the NVA assault on the ancient Vietnamese capital. At the end, 1,943 North Vietnamese have been killed. On the U.S. side, 142 marines were killed in action and 1,005 wounded.

MARCH 16 South Vietnam
Troops from the U.S. Army's Americal Division massacre more than 300 civilians, mostly women and children, in the village of My Lai.

APRIL 15 South Vietnam
Operation Pegasus ends with the relief and resupply of Khe Sanh, resulting in 1,011 reported enemy casualties with 51 U.S. Marines killed and 459 wounded.

MAY 13 France
Peace talks between North Vietnam, South Vietnam, and the United States begin in Paris. They want to solve the crisis in Vietnam and end the war.

MAY 22 South Vietnam
The U.S. Marine Corps makes its first use of the North American OV-10A "Bronco." It is an observation aircraft. It is also used for counterinsurgency operations. This means trying to find small groups of Viet Cong in the jungle, and then attacking them.

JUNE 5 United States
Senator Robert F. Kennedy is assassinated in Los Angeles, California. He is shot after winning the California Democratic primary for presidential candidate.

U.S. Marines under siege at the Khe Sanh base.

Observation aircraft – an aircraft that spies on the ground.

JUNE 27 South Vietnam

On General Westmoreland's orders, U.S. Marines begin to dismantle the base at Khe Sanh. It is then abandoned.

AUGUST 23 South Vietnam

Communist troops mount their third major offensive this year. They fire on 27 different Allied bases and cities, including Hue, the Da Nang Air Base, and Quang Tri City.

South Vietnamese troops pinned down by the Viet Cong.

AUGUST 24 United States

Amidst an army of anti-Vietnam War protesters, the Democratic Party meets in Chicago. It nominates Vice President Hubert H. Humphrey as its candidate. While the delegates convene inside, the antiwar protesters outside clash violently with Chicago police for nearly four days.

OCTOBER 31 United States

President Johnson announces a complete halt in both the aerial and naval bombardment of North Vietnam.

NOVEMBER 1 North Korea

North Vietnamese officials announce that they will meet in Paris with

TURNING POINTS: Khe Sanh

Khe Sanh (at right) was an American base near the border with North Vietnam. During the communist Tet Offensive it came under siege. It was defended by 6,000 U.S. Marines. The Americans were determined to defend it. If it fell, it would be a big victory for the North. Despite heavy communist attacks, the marines managed to hold on. Throughout the siege they were supplied by aircraft. Jets also dropped bombs on the attacking communists.

Bombardment – an attack using bombs.

EYEWITNESS:
John Larson, Qui Nhon, 1968

"Just as we hit the bunker all hell broke loose. There were about eight of us in there and scared to death as we heard the mortars and rockets continuing to land. This went on for hours. I just had to get a look at what was happening. So like a fool I got out of the bunker just far enough to see the closest thing I've seen to a vision of Hell. The sky was lit up like daytime and everywhere were dead VC. Something died in us that night."

NOVEMBER 11 South Vietnam
The U.S. Army's Americal Division ends Operation Wheeler/Wallowa after 14 months of battle. It results in 10,020 enemy casualties, with 683 U.S. Army personnel killed and 3,597 wounded.

NOVEMBER 26 France
President Johnson states that the forthcoming peace talks are to include people from the United States, South Vietnam, North Vietnam, and the Viet Cong.

DECEMBER 6 South Vietnam
Operation Henderson Hill ends, with 700 enemy casualties. Thirty-five U.S. Marines were killed and 273 wounded in action.

DECEMBER 29 South Vietnam
With the Tet Offensive fresh in their memories, the United States and South Vietnam announce that they will not honor any more holiday truces. The North Vietnamese and Viet Cong have lost 45,000 killed this year.

representatives from the United States, South Vietnam, and the Viet Cong to begin peace talks.

NOVEMBER 1 South Vietnam
South Vietnamese Army units, aided by American troops, launch an Accelerated Pacification Campaign. This is to regain the trust and control of the South Vietnamese villages that had been lost due to the major enemy offensives during the first part of the year. It is only partly successful.

NOVEMBER 5 United States
Vowing to bring "peace with honor" in Vietnam, Richard M. Nixon narrowly defeats Vice President Hubert H. Humphrey. He is elected president of the United States.

U.S Marines in a firefight with North Vietnamese troops.

Truce – an agreement by both sides to stop fighting.

Australian troops in Vietnam.

JANUARY 20, 1969, United States

Richard M. Nixon is inaugurated as president of the United States, succeeding Lyndon B. Johnson.

JANUARY 31 South Vietnam

U.S. military strength in South Vietnam numbers 539,800 men and women. The U.S. Marine Corps' strength, meanwhile, stands at 81,000 men and women.

FEBRUARY 16 South Vietnam

Allied forces observe a 24-hour ceasefire during Tet, the Vietnamese New Year. Despite the ceasefire, both Viet Cong and North Vietnamese Army (NVA) forces break the truce at least 203 times.

FEBRUARY 23 South Vietnam

Like the year before, communist forces launch attacks throughout South Vietnam. The attacks begin a day after the end of the seven-day truce for Tet. Rocket and mortar fire slams into Saigon. For nearly a week the enemy continue to launch attacks against a number of U.S. targets in the countryside and the cities.

FEBRUARY 27–28 South Vietnam

During Operation Dewey Canyon, the U.S. Marines make their biggest find of enemy arms and ammunition in the war to date. It includes four Russian 122mm howitzers, the first ever captured in the war.

TURNING POINTS: Tunnel warfare

A feature of the Vietnam War was the Viet Cong's use of tunnels. One of the largest tunnel networks was in the district of Cu Chi. At its peak the Cu Chi network covered 156 miles (250 km) from the Cambodian border. The tunnels contained beds, stores, kitchens, and hospitals. The Americans trained soldiers to crawl into the tunnels and fight the Viet Cong there. The soldiers were called Tunnel Rats. Today, some tunnels survive as tourist attractions.

Gunship – aircraft or helicopter armed with rockets and guns.

UH-1D helicopters of the U.S. 101st Airborne Division in action.

MARCH 19 South Vietnam
The Viet Cong and NVA launch 27 artillery and 13 ground attacks against military and civilian targets in the north of the country near the border.

APRIL 13 South Vietnam
To date, more Americans have been killed in Vietnam than during the Korean War. Vietnam has already cost the lives of 33,641 Americans since January 1961, compared to the 33,629 lost in Korea.

MARCH 1 South Vietnam
In Thua Thien Province, troops of the 101st Airborne Division (Airmobile) conduct Operation Kentucky Jumper. The U.S. paratroopers inflict 309 casualties on the enemy, while losing 61 soldiers dead and 409 wounded in action.

MARCH 2 South Vietnam
Village and hamlet elections are held throughout South Vietnam. The enemy makes no attempt to disrupt voting.

APRIL 23 United States
More than 250 student leaders from colleges in the United States make public statements. They say they will refuse being drafted into the armed forces as long as the war continues in Vietnam.

MAY 3 United States
The United States says that it will begin withdrawing its troops from Vietnam if the communists reduce their attacks against South Vietnamese targets.

EYEWITNESS: Eddie Dorrian, on board the USS *Kitty Hawk*

"The catapult hooks a plane by using a harness. A harness is a piece of steel cable about as thick as a baseball bat and as long as a couch. The plane has small hooks under the wings and each end of the harness is hooked up to each wing. The middle of the harness is then attached to the catapult. The catapult officer presses a button and releases the catapult, sending the plane off the ship and into the sky."

Howitzer – a type of field gun.

MAY 10 South Vietnam

Operation Apache Snow begins in the Da Krong Valley. U.S. paratroopers of the 101st Airborne Division capture the heavily protected "Hamburger Hill." It is called this because of all the blood spilt on it.

MAY 12 South Vietnam

The Viet Cong/North Vietnamese Army (NVA) strike throughout South Vietnam in some of the largest number of attacks since the Tet Offensive in 1968.

A soldier of the 101st Airborne Division on Hamburger Hill.

JUNE 8 United States

In a news conference, President Nixon announces the first troop withdrawals. A total of 25,000 will be brought home by the end of August. Nixon knows that the war is very unpopular at home.

JULY 20 United States

Race riots break out at the Marine Corps Base Camp Lejeune, North Carolina. White and black U.S. Marines fight, leaving one marine dead and another seriously injured.

AUGUST South Vietnam

Enemy activity throughout Vietnam increases due to the NVA and Viet Cong starting their "Autumn Campaign." This includes attacks on United States and South Vietnamese forces.

KEY PEOPLE: Students for a Democratic Society

In the 1960s this American student organization was against the Vietnam War. The students organized a march on Washington, D.C., in April 1965. The group became more militant, taking over university and college buildings. By 1969 the group had split into several groups. The most violent was the "Weathermen." They took part in terrorism. Other groups helped black radicals in the United States. With the end of the Vietnam War the organization ended.

Frontline – where fighting takes place.

EYEWITNESS: Wes Zanone, South Vietnam, 1969

"The Viet Cong unit knew we were coming. They couldn't take the baby, it would make too much noise, or maybe the mother wasn't strong enough to travel. So, they left them behind. The mother died but the baby lived. I think half the guys in the platoon volunteered to carry the baby down the hill. Having a baby in our midst gave new meaning to the war. We were protecting a totally innocent and helpless child, doing something worthwhile."

SEPTEMBER United States
Racial tensions again flare in the United States and in Vietnam. African-American marines protest over what they see as excessive force by guards at the Camp Pendleton prison. Tensions are also evident in Vietnam as well, though are not present in any of the frontline companies.

SEPTEMBER 2 North Vietnam
The President of North Vietnam, Ho Chi Minh, dies at his home in Hanoi, the capital, from heart failure.

OCTOBER 15 United States
Throughout the United States, Vietnam Moratoriums are held, protesting against the Vietnam War.

NOVEMBER 1 South Vietnam
Operation Toan Thang is launched. It results in 5,493 communist dead.

NOVEMBER 13–15 United States
Critics of the Vietnam War demonstrate in Washington, D.C. Protesters march from Arlington National Cemetery to the Capitol.

DECEMBER 1 United States
The first drawing of the draft lottery is conducted. Those l9-year-olds whose birthdate is September 14 and whose last name begins with a "J" will be the first to be called into the U.S. armed services. The lottery is very unpopular. Lots of young men try to dodge it. Some even go to Canada to escape being drafted.

Protesters against the Vietnam War in Washington, D.C.

Vietnam Moratorium – a demonstration against the Vietnam War.

Americans waiting to go back to the United States.

JANUARY 9, 1970, South Vietnam

In Pleiku, the soldiers of the U.S. Army's 4th Infantry Division find 30 storage huts. Inside the sheds is a huge supply of Viet Cong rice.

JANUARY 18 North Vietnam

A North Vietnamese spokesman says that they will allow American prisoners of war to send a postcard home once a month.

They will also allow them to receive packages from home every other month.

JANUARY 21 South Vietnam

American troops in Binh Long Province fight an unknown number of enemy soldiers 5 miles (8 km) northeast of Loc Ninh and 3 miles (4.8 km) from the Cambodian border. Communist forces are continually crossing the Cambodian border to attack American and Vietnamese targets.

JANUARY 26 South Vietnam

South Vietnamese President Nguyen Van Thieu appeals to all friendly nations for continued aid.

FEBRUARY 5 France

At the Paris Peace Talks, the North Vietnamese produce the first letter from a prisoner of war held in South Vietnam by the Viet Cong. The United States and South Vietnamese had placed great pressure on

KEY WEAPONS: Booby traps

Booby traps were used by the Viet Cong to delay enemy forces. The fear of booby traps created great stress among American soldiers. Booby traps included punji stakes, which were sharpened bamboo spikes (at right). The Viet Cong also used tripwires across paths. When someone walked into one, it would set off a grenade. This would often kill the victim. Booby traps were very difficult to spot in the jungle. They were certainly very effective weapons in Vietnam.

Punji stake – a sharpened piece of wood used in booby traps.

EYEWITNESS: Tom Haine, Mobile Riverine Force

"I stepped over the trench, walked up to the bunker, and dropped a fragmentation grenade. BOOM! We found out later that we had walked into a VC training camp. The VC that were left put the trainees up front to slow us down with sniper fire while they made their escape. This poor guy was probably too scared to shoot and was hiding in that bunker hoping we would just go away. He probably would have surrendered. He didn't need to die."

North Vietnamese delegates to account for the prisoners they hold.

FEBRUARY 17 United States
American President Richard M. Nixon states that the South Vietnamese are taking a greater role in fighting the war. This process is called Vietnamization.

MARCH 19 Cambodia
In Cambodia, Prince Norodom Sihanouk has been overthrown by General Lon Nol. General Lon Nol is a friend of the United States. However, he is a weak leader whose rule will be a disaster for Cambodia and its people.

APRIL 21 South Vietnam
President Thieu of South Vietnam says that the Vietnamese can gradually take greater control and responsibilities as the Americans withdraw from South Vietnam. He also says that South Vietnam needs more military and economic aid from its allies.

APRIL 29 Cambodia
South Vietnamese and U.S. Army forces carry out huge search and destroy operations in a dozen base areas in Cambodia. American boats also sweep up the Mekong Delta to reopen a supply line to Phnom Penh, the Cambodian capital.

APRIL 30 United States
There is a large public outcry in the U.S. against the American and South Vietnamese invasion of Cambodia.

U.S. troops and vehicles in Cambodia.

Sniper – a hidden rifleman who shoots at the enemy.

South Vietnamese read the results of the elections at the end of August.

dead are women and children. They also wound 60 seriously and destroy 156 houses.

JUNE 27 Cambodia

The last U.S. and South Vietnamese soldiers leave Cambodia. Some 4,764 enemy have been killed. In addition, 9,081 rifles, 1,283 machine guns, and thousands of sacks of rice have been captured or destroyed. U.S casualties are 399 killed and 1,501 wounded.

AUGUST 20 South Vietnam

A U.S. Department of Defense study reports on the use of illegal drugs by U.S. servicemen during the Vietnam war. It concludes that about three out of every ten U.S. servicemen who are interviewed have either smoked marijuana or taken other illegal drugs in Vietnam.

MAY 4 United States

As the U.S. and South Vietnamese raid into Cambodia continues, college campuses explode in a wave of antiwar protesting. At Kent State University in Kent, Ohio, National Guardsmen kill four students.

JUNE 11 South Vietnam

The Viet Cong kill 74 civilians to terrorize the villagers of Phou Thanh. Many of the

AUGUST 30 South Vietnam

In elections held throughout South Vietnam, 30 South Vietnamese senators are

KEY WEAPON: Huey helicopter

In the 1950s the U.S Army wanted a helicopter that could carry out many tasks. The result was the Bell UH-1, better known as the "Huey." The first Hueys began arriving in Vietnam in 1963. Before the end of the Vietnam War 5,000 were in service. They were used for a wide variety of tasks. They could take off and land without the need for an airfield. This made them very useful for jungle operations. Hueys were also used as helicopter gunships in Vietnam.

Helicopter gunship – helicopter armed with rockets and bombs.

EYEWITNESS: Major Shorack, A-1 Skyraider pilot

"The only apprehension you feel is when you roll in on a target from which you know they are firing on you. Then you make yourself as small as possible and crouch in the cockpit. Dive-bombing isn't bad, because you stay high. When napalming you come down low and fly level at about 100 feet. Napalm is jellied gasoline that we drop on the Viet Cong to burn them. It's nasty stuff, but they are nasty and this is war."

elected. There are many attacks by the Viet Cong against the voters. Forty-two civilians are killed.

OCTOBER 8 South Vietnam
American commanders in Vietnam complete their plans to send a further 40,000 troops back home to the United States. They will be home by the end of this year. This will leave a total of 344,000 U.S. troops in South Vietnam.

NOVEMBER 19 North Vietnam
U.S. Special Forces conduct a joint raid aimed at the Son Tay Prisoner of War Camp, 20 miles (32 km) west of Hanoi, in order to liberate Americans held by the North Vietnamese. Apparently, the North Vietnamese had been tipped off beforehand and had moved the prisoners.

NOVEMBER 21 United States
U.S. Secretary of Defense Melvin R. Laird announces the unsuccessful helicopter raid on Son Tay.

DECEMBER 3 South Vietnam
American military strength in Vietnam is down to 349,700, the lowest number since October 29, 1966.

DECEMBER 10 United States
President Richard M. Nixon is angry that North Vietnamese forces have increased their level of fighting in South Vietnam as the American forces withdraw. If they do not stop, he will resume bombing targets within North Vietnam.

U.S. National Guardsmen confront demonstrators against the Vietnam War at Ohio State University in Columbus.

National Guard – part-time soldier.

JANUARY, 1971, South Vietnam

Communist activity is down. In January 1970, Allied forces sighted 4,425 enemy troops. By December 1970, the Allies recorded only 4,159 sightings of the enemy.

JANUARY 6 South Vietnam

U.S. Secretary of Defense Melvin R. Laird says that "Vietnamization" is running well ahead of schedule. Combat missions by U.S. troops will end the following summer.

JANUARY 11 South Vietnam

U.S. Marine Operation Upshur Stream is conducted in and around "Charlie Ridge." This is near Da Nang in the so-called "rocket belt." Contacts with the 575th North Vietnamese Artillery Battalion result in 13 enemy being killed.

FEBRUARY 8 Laos

President Thieu announces that some units of South Vietnamese troops have gone into Laos. They have done this to destroy enemy supply routes and troop concentrations. At this point, no American troops or advisors working with the South Vietnamese have so far crossed the border into Laos.

MARCH 2 Laos

The South Vietnamese Marine Brigade 147 makes a helicopter assault into Laos.

U.S. troops prepare to leave Vietnam.

KEY WEAPON: Agent Orange

In Vietnam the Americans used Agent Orange, a herbicide, to kill vegetation. This was to prevent the enemy being able to hide in trees and bushes. During the war the Americans dropped hundreds of thousands of gallons of Agent Orange from aircraft. Unfortunately, Agent Orange contained poison and made those who came into contact with it sick. Many Americans and Vietnamese later developed cancer because of contact with Agent Orange.

Agent Orange – chemical used by the Americans to clear jungle.

President Thieu of South Vietnam.

the 38th NVA Regiment from these hamlets after four days of savage fighting.

APRIL 7–12 South Vietnam

So as not to give the impression that the United States has given up on its South Vietnamese ally, the U.S. 1st Marine Regiment launches a five-day offensive, called Operation Scott Orchard. This is in the area west of An Hoa. The U.S. Marines suffer few casualties.

APRIL 29 South Vietnam

At the U.S. Embassy compound in Saigon, Ambassador Ellsworth Bunker presents E Company, Marine Security Guard Detachment, with the "Meritorious Unit Commendation." The Marine Security Guards played a key role in the defense of the U.S. embassy in Saigon in January 1968 during the Tet Offensive. (During that battle they recaptured the embassy from the Viet Cong.) They will do so again when the Americans leave the embassy for the last time in 1975.

MARCH 24 United States

The U.S. Department of Defense announces that the North Vietnamese have started to move Russian-supplied artillery into the Demilitarized Zone (DMZ).

MARCH 29 South Vietnam

The 38th North Vietnamese Regiment surfaces from its mountain hideouts near An Hoa. It attacks Duc Duc, Phu Da, and Thu Bon hamlets. However, the 51st South Vietnamese Regiment fights back. It expels

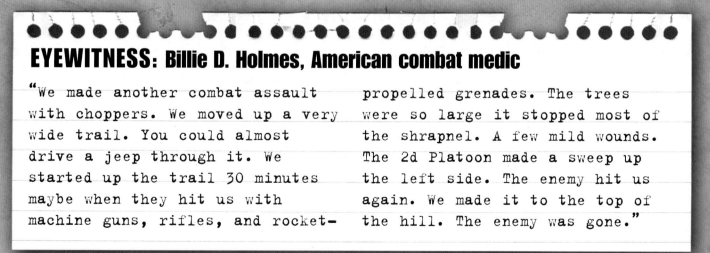

EYEWITNESS: Billie D. Holmes, American combat medic

"We made another combat assault with choppers. We moved up a very wide trail. You could almost drive a jeep through it. We started up the trail 30 minutes maybe when they hit us with machine guns, rifles, and rocket-propelled grenades. The trees were so large it stopped most of the shrapnel. A few mild wounds. The 2d Platoon made a sweep up the left side. The enemy hit us again. We made it to the top of the hill. The enemy was gone."

DMZ – Demilitarized Zone, the border between North and South Vietnam.

A U.S. Air Force F-4 Phantom jet.

North Carolina, are sent to Washington, D.C. They will assist the police in controlling antiwar protesters.

MAY 12 South Vietnam

Operation Imperial Lake takes place. This is the last major U.S. Marine operation in Vietnam. It ends with 305 North vietnamese Army/Viet Cong killed. The U.S.Marines lose 24 killed in combat operations.

JUNE 4 South Vietnam

The 3rd Marine Amphibious Brigade turns over its last bases in Vietnam to the U.S. Army at Camp Books.

APRIL 30 United States

U.S. President Richard M. Nixon welcomes home the 1st Marine Division at Camp Pendleton, California. The last marine aircraft left Vietnam in April.

MAY 3–4 United States

Marines from the U.S. Marine Corps Base, Quantico, Virginia, and Camp Lejeune,

JUNE 21 South Vietnam

American units continue to move back to bases in the United States and throughout Asia. The U.S. military strength in South Vietnam is now down to 244,900 men and women. For the United States the end of the war in Vietnam appears to be in sight.

KEY PEOPLE: Black soldiers

American involvement in Vietnam resulted in greater African-American participation in the army. Civil rights campaigner Martin Luther King complained that black youths in the army were more likely to take part in the fighting. While true, the Vietnam War changed the U.S. armed forces for the better. African-Americans reenlisted at higher rates than did whites. Also, the percentage of African-American officers doubled between 1964 and 1967.

F-4 Phantom – American warplane

EYEWITNESS: Khan Truing, South Vietnamese soldier

"At about the same time, on the hills of A Luoi, the enemy had overrun us, and artillery was called to fire on our own position. Men seriously wounded were left behind, becoming targets for artillery fire. The lightly wounded rushed to open ground, waiting for airlift by helicopters. There were too many soldiers; they fought each other to get on the helicopter, to hold on to the skids. I hate war. I detest war."

JULY 9–11 China
U.S. National Security Advisor, Dr. Henry A. Kissinger, visits the People's Republic of China. This is in preparation for President Nixon's historic trip to China. He was the first U.S. president to visit the country.

JULY 12 South Vietnam
American troop strength in South Vietnam stands at 236,000. It is decreasing at a rate of about 14,000 men per month.

AUGUST 18 South Vietnam
Both Australia and New Zealand announce the withdrawal of their troops from Southeast Asia.

OCTOBER 3 South Vietnam
President Nguyen Van Thieu is reelected president for another four-year term. The election is marked by protests and Viet Cong violence.

NOVEMBER 12 United States
President Richard M. Nixon announces that American forces are now taking a purely defensive role in Vietnam. Only the South Vietnamese will be conducting offensive military operations from now on.

NOVEMBER 26 North Vietnam
Angry over North Vietnam's stalling at the Paris Peace Talks, President Nixon authorizes more bombing of North Vietnam.

DECEMBER 31 South Vietnam
To date, 45,626 Americans have been killed in action while on duty in South Vietnam.

South Vietnamese soldiers on patrol.

Skids – helicopter landing feet.

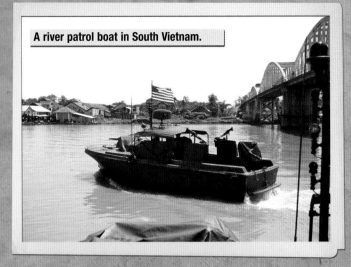

A river patrol boat in South Vietnam.

JANUARY 12, 1972, Laos

The communist forces in Laos capture the city of Long Chen. They are using Soviet-supplied tanks and artillery.

JANUARY 25 South Vietnam

A new American–South Vietnamese peace initiative is announced by presidents Nixon and Nguyen Van Thieu. They want to bring an end to the war in Vietnam.

FEBRUARY 21 China

President Nixon arrives in the People's Republic of China. He meets with Chinese leaders, including Mao Zedong and Chou En Lai. In an effort to win peace in Vietnam, America says it will reduce U.S. troops in Taiwan. President Nixon in turn asks China to press upon the North Vietnamese leaders that the time for peace is now.

MARCH 10 Cambodia

Lon Nol makes himself president of Cambodia. He is an ally of the United States.

MARCH 10 South Vietnam

The U.S. 101st Airborne Division withdraws from South Vietnam. It is the last American division to leave South Vietnam.

MARCH 23 France

The Paris Peace Talks are suspended by the U.S. delegation. They inform the North Vietnamese that they will be resumed only

KEY PEOPLE: Richard Nixon

Republican Richard Nixon became U.S. president in 1968. Under his policy of "Vietnamization," combat roles were transferred to South Vietnamese troops. However, he ordered an invasion of Cambodia in 1970. This caused widespread protests in the U.S. An agreement to end the war in Vietnam was reached at Paris in January 1973. All American military personnel left Vietnam. Nixon had played his part in ending America's longest war. He died in April 1994.

Division – a unit of 5,000 to 10,000 soldiers.

● ●

EYEWITNESS: Mike Austin, Cobra gunship pilot

"The strangest, and probably most fearsome, was the flechette rocket or 'nail.' Each warhead contains 2,200 steel nails with fins stamped on one end, resembling tiny darts. After the solid-fuel motor propelled the rocket to supersonic speed in under two seconds, the warhead exploded. The shower of nails hit the ground over the size of a football field."

when North Vietnam is serious about discussing specific issues.

MARCH 30 South Vietnam

A major North Vietnamese offensive begins. It is called the Easter Offensive. The total U.S. military strength in the South is 95,000 military personnel. Only 6,000 are combat troops. The North Vietnamese Army (NVA) attacks on three fronts. It pours across the border from North Vietnam. Quang Tri, South Vietnam's northernmost province, is under threat.

APRIL 7 North Vietnam

As the Easter Offensive continues, the U.S. bombing of North Vietnam resumes.

APRIL 15 North Vietnam

The bombing of Hanoi and Haiphong in North Vietnam starts again for the first time since 1968.

APRIL 15–20 United States

A wave of protests takes place in the United States. This is a result of the increase in fighting in Southeast Asia. The protests begin at the University of Maryland. Eight hundred National Guardsmen are ordered onto the campus. And 400 students are arrested at the University of Florida. Hundreds more protesting students are arrested across the country.

APRIL 22 United States

There are massive peace protests across the country. Around 60,000 people march in Washington alone.

South Korean troops in Vietnam.

Warhead – explosive tip of rocket.

A refugee camp in South Vietnam.

MAY 4 France
The Paris talks are again suspended indefinitely by the American and South Vietnamese delegations. The reason is a "complete lack of progress."

MAY 8 North Vietnam
Haiphong and other North Vietnamese harbors are mined by the U.S. Navy. The mining and aerial bombing will only stop when all U.S. prisoners of war are returned and an international ceasefire begins.

APRIL 23 South Vietnam
The North Vietnamese Army (NVA) captures the city of Dak To. So far, 250,000 South Vietnamese civilians have fled their homes.

JULY 13 France
The Paris Peace Talks resume after a 10-week break. A solution to the situation in Vietnam is even more pressing.

APRIL 27 South Vietnam
A major NVA attack occurs against Quang Tri City. The North Vietnamese are using Soviet-supplied tanks. Casualties among South Vietnamese troops are heavy.

SEPTEMBER 16 South Vietnam
Quang Tri City is recaptured by South Vietnamese forces. The massive support from American aircraft is helping the South defeat the Easter Offensive.

TURNING POINTS: Bombing North Vietnam

The United States launched bombing raids against North Vietnam starting in 1965. American pilots were not allowed to bomb civilian targets. However, they did knock out bridges, railroads, and military targets. As time went on the bombings demoralized the people of the North. The destruction of railroads meant the North had problems getting food to its cities. The bombing campaign in 1972 was a factor that led to the peace agreement in 1973.

"Iron Triangle" – nickname of Viet Cong base near Saigon.

EYEWITNESS: Richard Shand, U.S. tank driver

"We fire perhaps five clips—20 rounds, really far fewer than we should have, but we stop when the VC barrage in front of us halts abruptly. Echoes fade, the smoke clears, and the ringing in my ears subsides. Purple after-images of the bright tracer flashes remain burnt into my retina. The following morning the infantry swept the area in front of our position. The VC had run away so fast that they had left unfired weapons behind."

OCTOBER 8 France
A breakthrough in the Paris Peace Talks. One of North Vietnam's senior leaders, Le Duc Tho, has agreed for the first time that South Vietnam can remain in existence. After a ceasefire it can negotiate with North Vietnam for a political settlement.

NOVEMBER 7 United States
In the presidential elections, President Richard Nixon is reelected president of the United States. He has defeated Senator George McGovern.

NOVEMBER 11 South Vietnam
Direct U.S. Army participation in the Vietnam War ends. The large base at Long Binh is given back to the South Vietnamese.

NOVEMBER 20–21 France
More private talks are held between Dr. Henry Kissinger and Le Duc Tho, the North Vietnamese negotiator. They are to reach a final peace agreement over Vietnam.

DECEMBER 13 France
Talks between Dr. Kissinger and Le Duc Tho reach a standstill. The South has demanded that North Vietnam withdraws its troops from the South.

DECEMBER 18 North Vietnam
Because the peace talks in Paris have stalled again, President Nixon orders air attacks against Hanoi and Haiphong. These are known as the "Christmas Bombings." They cause much damage in the North.

A North Vietnamese bridge bombed by the Americans.

Infantry – foot soldiers.

American troops leaving Saigon.

FEBRUARY 21 Laos

A ceasefire is agreed in Laos.

MARCH 27 South Vietnam

This is the last day of the 60-day ceasefire period. The North Vietnamese have been releasing American prisoners of war. The United States turns over its military bases to the South Vietnamese. It withdraws its forces from South Vietnam.

JANUARY 27, 1973, France

Representatives of the United States, the Republic of Vietnam (South Vietnam), the Democratic Republic of Vietnam (North Vietnam), and the Viet Cong sign a peace agreement in Paris.

JUNE 13 France

The United States, South Vietnam, and North Vietnam, as well as representatives from the Viet Cong, sign a starting agreement to put the Paris Peace Accords into effect. Peace now seems to have arrived in Vietnam.

JANUARY 28 South Vietnam

The final withdrawal of Allied forces from South Vietnam begins.

JULY 1 United States

The new financial year begins with a large reduction of American assistance to South Vietnam. Military aid goes from $2.2 billion

TURNING POINTS: Paris Peace Accords

The peace accords were signed in January 1973. They brought an immediate ceasefire throughout North and South Vietnam. All U.S. bases in the South would be dismantled, and all foreign troops would withdraw from Cambodia and Laos. Vietnam would remain divided until the country was reunited by "peaceful means." Unfortunately, the North and South later accused each other of breaking the truce. Fighting between the two broke out again. At right are Americans at the Paris Peace Accords.

Prisoner of war – a soldier who has been captured by the enemy.

EYEWITNESS: Captain Lu, South Vietnamese Army

"As the planes left, I stood motionless, watching, until the last plane full of U.S. troops took off. In those days I felt that sooner or later something would happen to my country. The malicious smile of the NVA representative when he had supervised the withdrawal of U.S. forces kept coming back to my mind. The ever-increasing bureaucracy, corruption, and bribery were the main causes of the people's dissatisfaction."

to $1.1 billion. Many now doubt whether South Vietnam can survive without massive American aid.

JULY 30 South Vietnam
Fewer than 250 U.S. military personnel remain in South Vietnam. This is the maximum number allowed by the Paris Peace Accords.

AUGUST United States
A U.S. district court rules the secret war in Cambodia "unconstitutional." It issues an injunction against the Nixon Administration's right to wage it. However, a lower court issues a delay against this injunction.

AUGUST 14 United States
Congress declares the end of U.S.-funded military actions in Southeast Asia.

OCTOBER United States
The U.S. Congress passes the War Powers Act. This is designed to limit the ability of the president to wage war without Congressional approval. This is to stop events like the invasion of Cambodia, which angered many Americans.

DECEMBER 15 South Vietnam
Under the terms of the Paris Peace Accords, a Joint Military Commission (JMC) was set up. This contained members of both sides in the war. The commission was to help bring peace to Vietnam. Today, a JMC unit is ambushed by communist troops. A U.S. soldier is killed and several are wounded.

South Vietnamese prisoners released by North Vietnam.

Military aid – weapons given to another country.

A forlorn memorial outside Saigon.

THE NOBLE SACRIFICE OF ALLIED SOLDIERS WILL NEVER BE FORGOTTEN

Committee offices in the Watergate Hotel, Washington, D.C., were burgled in June 1971. Later it was proved that the burglars had been hired by Nixon's Committee to Re-Elect the President.

AUGUST 9 United States
Nixon is succeeded in office by Vice President Gerald R. Ford. Ford tells the American nation today: "Our long national nightmare is over."

DECEMBER 13 South Vietnam
With over 20 divisions, the North Vietnamese Army (NVA) begins a new offensive against South Vietnam. The NVA is supported by Soviet-supplied tanks. It is very strong. Its leaders believe they can conquer the South.

DECEMBER 31 South Vietnam
NVA units encircle Phuoc Long City (Song Be), capital of Phuoc Long Province. The city is near the Cambodian border.

JULY 1, 1974, United States
American aid to South Vietnam continues to go down. Funding for South Vietnamese military forces is set at $700 million, down from $1.1 billion.

AUGUST 8 United States
Caught up in the Watergate scandal, President Richard M. Nixon, the 35th President of the United States, is forced to resign from office. The Democratic National

KEY PEOPLE: Henry Kissinger

Henry Kissinger was an expert in security issues. He was appointed as assistant for national security affairs by President Nixon in 1968. He became secretary of state in 1973. At first he proposed a hardline policy in Vietnam. However, later he wanted to negotiate with the North. In 1973, after months of talks, he brought about a ceasefire in Vietnam. For this achievement he was awarded a joint Nobel Prize for Peace with North Vietnam's Le Duc Tho.

Nobel Prize for Peace – an award for someone who works for peace.

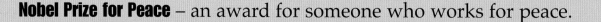

JANUARY 7, 1975, South Vietnam
The NVA captures Phuoc Long Province.

MARCH 10 South Vietnam
The NVA attacks Ban Me Thuot at the start of its 1975 Spring Offensive.

MARCH 24 South Vietnam
Quang Ngai City and Tam Ky falls to the advancing NVA. The next day, Hue City falls to the NVA.

Vietnamese civilians flee Saigon in April 1975.

APRIL 21 South Vietnam
President Nguyen Van Thieu resigns as President of South Vietnam. He flees to Taiwan. He leaves control to his vice president, Tran Van Huong.

APRIL 28 South Vietnam
General Duong Van "Big" Minh becomes the last president of South Vietnam.

APRIL 29 South Vietnam
U.S. Marines carry out Operation Frequent Wind. This is the evacuation of Americans, foreign nationals, and various Vietnamese officials and citizens from Saigon. They are carried to ships of the U.S. Seventh Fleet lying off the coast of South Vietnam. Many Vietnamese people are left behind.

APRIL 30 South Vietnam
The NVA enters Saigon (now named Ho Chi Minh City) and arrests General Minh. Organized South Vietnamese resistance now collapses. The long conflict in Vietnam is finally over.

EYEWITNESS: Colonel David Hackworth, U.S. Army

"The Vietnam War was a disaster from its bad beginning until its tragic end. It killed four million Vietnamese and 58,000 Americans. Millions more, Vietnamese and Americans, were wounded by shell or shock, and the war came close to ripping our country asunder. With the exception of the Civil War, no war wrought such long-term damage to the American soul. Did our military learn from the tragic lesson of Vietnam? The mistakes were all buried."

Evacuation – to leave a city or country in a hurry.

Glossary

Agent Orange: chemical used by the Americans to clear jungle

airborne: refers to soldiers who are parachutists

airmobile troops: soldiers who ride in helicopters

artillery: cannons or mortars

ARVN: Army of the Republic of Vietnam

battalion: a unit of 500 soldiers

body count: the number of enemy killed, wounded, or captured during an operation

booby trap: a hidden trap that is intended to wound or kill

ceasefire: a halt in the fighting

"Charlie": the Viet Cong; the enemy

Chinook: CH-47 cargo helicopter

Cobra: an AH-1G helicopter gunship

compound: a fortified military place

contact: firing on or being fired upon by the enemy

DMZ: Demilitarized Zone, the dividing line between North and South Vietnam established in 1954 at the Geneva Convention

draft: to make citizens become members of the armed forces

F-4: Phantom jet fighter-bomber

fire base: temporary artillery base used for fire support of ground troops

Free World forces: the soldiers from other countries who fought on the side of South Vietnam

friendly fire: accidental attacks on U.S. or Allied soldiers by other U.S. or Allied soldiers

frontline: where fighting takes place

Green Beret: a member of the U.S. Special Forces unit

ground troops: soldiers who usually fight on the ground

"Grunt": nickname for a U.S. soldier

guerrilla: a soldier who does not wear a uniform and fights behind the lines

gunship: aircraft or helicopter armed with rockets and guns

howitzer: a type of field gun

infantry: foot soldiers

military aid: weapons, vehicles, and aircraft given to another country

military coup: revolt by soldiers

napalm: a fuel and gel mixture used in bombs that are dropped from aircraft

NVA: North Vietnamese Army

observation aircraft: an aircraft that spies on the ground

POW: prisoner of war

punji stake: a sharpened piece of wood used in booby traps

sniper: a hidden rifleman who shoots at the enemy

sortie: a mission flown by a warplane

tactic: plan

Vietnamization: U.S. policy started by President Richard Nixon late in the war to turn over the fighting to the South Vietnamese

warhead: explosive tip of a rocket

Further resources

BOOKS ABOUT THE VIETNAM WAR

Vietnam War by DK Publishing, DK Children, 2005

Vietnam War (A First Book) by John Devaney, Franklin Watts, 1993

10,000 Days of Thunder: A History of the Vietnam War by Philip Caputo, Atheneum, 2005

The Vietnam War: A History in Documents by Marilyn B. Young, John J. Fitzgerald, and Tom Grunfeld, Oxford University Press, USA, 2003

Vietnam War Battles & Leaders (Battles and Leaders) by Stuart Murray, DK Children, 2004

Fighting the Vietnam War (On the Front Line) by Brian Fitzgerald, Raintree, 2006

USEFUL WEBSITES

www.vietnampix.com

www.pbs.org/battlefieldvietnam

www.historyplace.com/unitedstates/vietnam

www.spartacus.schoolnet.co.uk/vietnam.html

http://vietnam.vassar.edu

www.vietnamwar.net

Index